Travel Quiz

Travel Quiz is a book for all travellers, whether by train, plane, car, bus or even on foot. There are questions on all aspects of travel, including picture puzzles, recognition games, anagrams, general knowledge, geography, history, architecture, costume and food. It will provide hours of fun for the whole family, and of course all the questions are answered at the back of the book if you are stuck.

Travel Quiz

John Meirion

Beaver Books

Published by
The Hamlyn Publishing Group Limited
London · New York · Sydney · Toronto
Astronaut House, Feltham, Middlesex, England
First published 1976
Reprinted 1976

© Copyright Text J. M. Thomas 1976
© Copyright Illustrations
The Hamlyn Publishing Group Limited 1976
ISBN 0 600 38740 2

Printed in England by
Cox & Wyman Limited
London, Reading and Fakenham
Set in Monotype Garamond

Line drawings by Mike Bell
Cover illustration by Mike Bell

Contents

About this Quiz

Everybody travels somewhere at some time – on holiday, to work, to school, or perhaps to visit friends and relations. Then there are other people's travels – those we read about in books and magazines, watch on films and television, and hear about from travellers at first hand; or the travelling we can watch others doing when a train roars past, an airliner takes off, a ship sails away, or our friends leave in their car to go on holiday.

Travel Quiz is about all kinds of travel and has a wide assortment of questions, pictures and puzzles. You can tackle them in a number of ways, perhaps by using your own general knowledge; or by looking up the answers in a book (you are most certainly 'allowed' to do so as this is a quiz and not a school examination!). Another idea is to test your friends and your family, and *Travel Quiz* can be used sometimes when you are actually travelling.

Really, then, you can try to answer the questions in any way you like and, in case you would like to refer to some books, a few titles are mentioned below. You may even want to go on and make up some of your own extra travel questions, but don't forget to provide the answers also.

Useful Books

ABC World Airways Guide It appears each month in two fat volumes and contains an amazing amount of information about airlines, times, fares and distances. You can't buy it easily, but travel agents often throw it away when the new one comes out; so, if you ask a travel agent politely, he may give you an old copy.

AA and *RAC Handbooks* There are thousands of these around in homes, libraries and schools. Even an out-of-date one can be very useful for basic information.

ABC Railway Guide and *Bradshaws Railway Guide* These are interesting guides containing timetables and other railway information in Britain.

Train, plane, coach and holiday brochures are nearly always free from travel agents. There are also hundreds of other guides and books about travel at home and abroad. You can also answer questions in *Travel Quiz* by looking up books in your library.

Great sights

If you have travelled by plane or train or car or ship to see these, where are you?

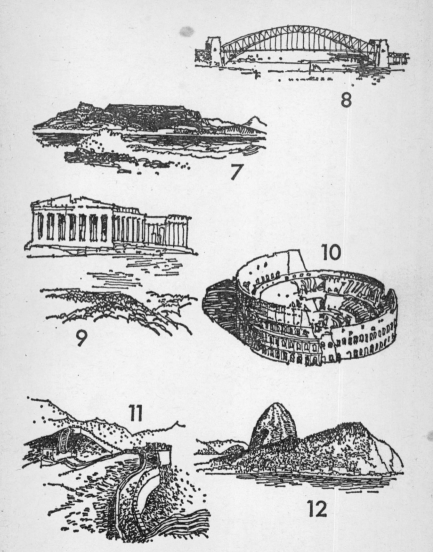

8

7

10

9

11

12

Travel words

As a traveller you might come across these words or phrases. What do they mean?

1 Passport
2 Travellers' cheque
3 Crossing the line
4 Immigration
5 Quarantine
6 Lifeboat drill
7 Crossing the bar
8 Visa
9 Customs *and* Douane
10 Greenwich Mean Time
11 International Date Line
12 Travel sickness
13 Poste restante
14 Equator
15 Latitude
16 Longitude
17 Mayday
18 Port health authority

True or false?

Which of these statements is true and which false?

1 A gallon of petrol in the US is the same measure as that in Britain.

2 In Japan everybody eats food with chopsticks.

3 In Australia traffic is driven on the left as in Britain.

4 You can bring your pet dog or cat into Britain without its having to go into quarantine if you can prove it has not been in contact with any other animal.

5 The city of Venice is sinking into the sea.

6 Some passengers can travel on nearly every major airline for nothing.

7 The British railwaymen's uniform red ties are related to the clothing of the earliest railwaymen.

8 A nautical mile is the same as the statute mile used for land measurement.

9 Cars' engines are measured in horsepower as the result of a test made on the strongest horses in the nineteenth century.

10 The Elephant and Castle in London is called this because an elephant once lived in a castle at that spot.

Airliners

What are the names or numbers of these modern aircraft?

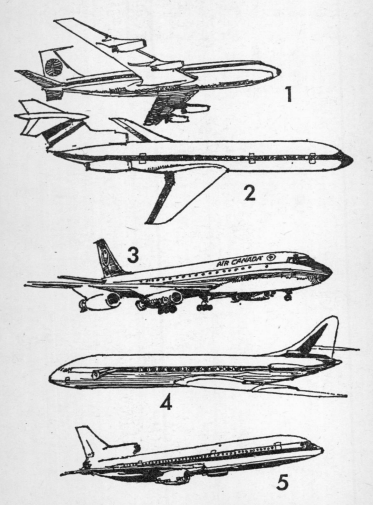

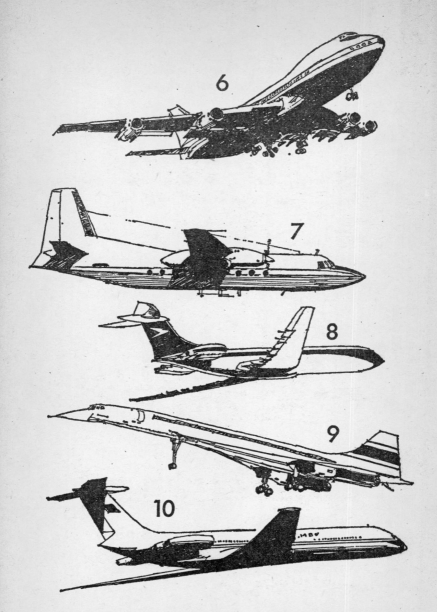

Famous stations and famous trains

A In which famous cities are these main-line stations?

1 Temple Meads
2 St Pancras
3 Lime Street
4 City
5 Paddington
6 Waverley

7 St David's
8 Piccadilly
9 Exchange
10 Spa
11 Central
12 New Street

B Between which cities did, or do, these famous trains run?

1 Orient Express
2 Flying Scotsman
3 Cornish Riviera Limited
4 Blue Train
5 Bristolian

6 Super Chief
7 Mistral
8 Rheingold
9 Master Cutler
10 Fensman

Crazy map

Somebody does not know his geography, as every one of these names of seaside towns is wrong. Can you switch the names to their correct positions without looking at the answers?

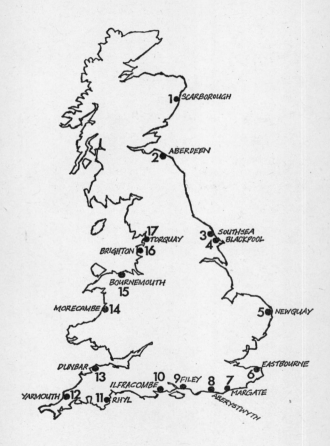

Capital fun

A What are the capital cities of these countries?

1 France
2 Spain
3 Egypt
4 USA
5 Britain
6 Australia
7 Nigeria
8 Irish Republic
9 Sweden
10 Switzerland
11 USSR
12 India

B Of what countries are these the capitals?

1 Pretoria
2 Oslo
3 Brussels
4 Rome
5 Ankara
6 Lisbon
7 Algiers
8 Nairobi
9 Tokyo
10 Vienna
11 The Hague
12 Prague

Puzzle cars

Here are some famous car names – but the letters need to be rearranged!

1 DOFR
2 ARGAUJ
3 OVVOL
4 SHLYCERR
5 UXLVAHAL
6 EVORR
7 SORMIR
8 OCTIENR
9 REECDSME
10 TLUNARE
11 AFTI
12 NOLVKSEWGA

Uniforms around the world

Here are some famous uniforms which travellers see. To which countries do they belong?

Odd loco

Which one of these locomotives is different from the others?

Money around the world

In which countries would you use these units of money? (Remember that in some cases more than one country uses the same word.)

1 Franc

2 Yen

3 Peseta

4 Mark

5 Guilder

6 Dollar

7 Rand

8 Schilling

9 Pound

10 Drachma

11 Dinar

12 Kroner

13 Lira

14 Escudo

15 Markka

16 Rupee

17 Rouble

18 Krone

Famous travellers – real and fictional

1 In a famous story written 100 years ago, two travellers went on a journey round the world.
   (a) What was the title of the book?
   (b) What were the travellers' names?
   (c) Where did they start their journey?
   (d) What kind of vehicles did they use for different parts of the journey?

2 In the fourteenth century a boy and his cat went on the long walk to London. What was the boy's name and what happened to him?

3 Who travelled from Italy to China in the thirteenth century?

4 Who were the first men to walk on the Moon, and when?

5 Who wrote the thriller *Murder on the Orient Express*?

6 Who flew the first aeroplane across the Channel, and when?

7 Who was the famous murderer, travelling to Canada, who was caught on an Atlantic liner in 1910?

8 Who wrote *Travels with a Donkey* and said 'I travel not to go anywhere, but to go. I travel for travel's sake'? (He also wrote a famous book for children about a one-legged pirate.)

Airports

In which country are these airports and which cities do they serve?

1 Orly
2 Hellinikon
3 Kennedy
4 Schiphol
5 Bandaranaike
6 Tempelhof
7 Heathrow
8 Haneda
9 O'Hare
10 Cointrin

11 Leonardo da Vinci
12 Dorval International
13 Paya Lebar
14 Kingsford Smith
15 Ikeja
16 Santa Cruz
17 Mehrabad
18 Dum Dum
19 D. F. Malan
20 Ben Gurion International

Odd vehicles

Here are some strange vehicles which you might travel in or see on your travels. What are their correct names?

Railway words

Here are some questions about common words, letters and phrases used in connection with railways.

1 What does *Inter City* mean?

2 What is a *Freightliner*?

3 Railwaymen often talk about the *up line* and the *down line*; what do they mean?

4 *Standard gauge* is a railway measurement. What is it and what does it refer to?

5 A train has a *headcode*. What is it?

6 What is *continuous braking*?

7 Some passengers use a *season* ticket and others might use a *cheap day* ticket. What are they?

8 A train might run over an *unattended crossing* and you might go across it in a car. What is it?

9 You might hear a signalman talking about a train's *road*. What would he be talking about?

10 SR, LNER, GWR, LMS. On some stations in Britain you can still see these initials on gates, seats and notices and also on pictures of old locomotives and rolling stock, but what do they mean?

Motoring words

A All these words have something to do with the working of a car. What are they?

1 Disc brakes

2 Gears

3 Speedometer

4 Overdrive

5 Cylinder

6 Sparking plug

7 Carburettor

8 Starter

9 Distributor

10 Alternator

11 Ammeter

12 Differential

B All these words have something to do with motoring, though not with the engine of a car. What do they mean?

1 Road Fund licence

2 Radial and crossply

3 Rally

4 Jack

5 Underpass

6 Understeer

7 Hard shoulder

8 Lighting-up time

9 Gran Turismo

10 Green card

Famous sights

You have just travelled (by car or train or bus or legs) to see these famous sights. What, then, are you looking at?

1

2

3

4

5

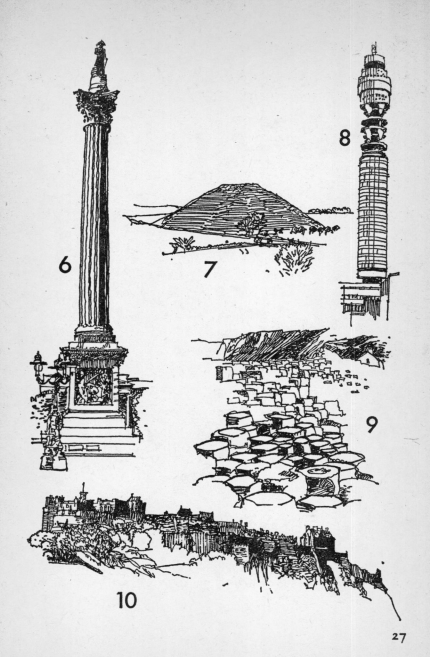

6

7

8

9

10

Food around the world

A Some towns or countries are famous for certain foods, which are best eaten there. So where would you go to eat these?

1 Hot dog

2 Fondue

3 Roast beef

4 Sachertorte

5 Bouillabaisse

6 Spare ribs

7 Spaghetti

8 Wiener Schnitzel

9 Moussaka

10 Smorgasbord

11 Sauerkraut

12 Curry

13 Truffles

14 Birds' nest soup

B If you like cheese you will know where these famous cheeses come from.

1 Parmesan

2 Cheddar

3 Edam

4 Camembert

5 Dunlop

6 Caboc

7 Gruyère

8 Feta

9 Gorgonzola

10 Roquefort

Odd car out

Which of these pictures is different from the other five?

In a foreign language

A In which language do you say 'Thank you' like this?

1 Gracias
2 Dank U zeer
3 Grazie
4 Stisibo

5 Merci
6 Tack så mycket
7 Obrigado
8 Danke

B What do these words mean, and in what languages?

1 Oui
2 Ja
3 Si
4 Niet
5 Non

6 S'il vous plaît
7 Per favore
8 Bitte
9 Hommes and Dames
10 Damen and Herren

Motoring initials

A What do these motoring club initials stand for?

1 AA
2 RAC
3 TCF
4 ADAC

5 TCS
6 RACE
7 ÖAMTC
8 TCI

B What countries do these International Registration letters stand for?

1 N
2 NL
3 F
4 GR
5 D

6 GB
7 CDN
8 L
9 M
10 YU

C What are the letters for these countries?

1 Belgium
2 Sweden
3 Switzerland
4 Hungary
5 United States of America

6 Italy
7 Jersey
8 Spain
9 Finland
10 Portugal

Vintage airliners

These are some old airliners of the 1930s and 1940s. Can you name them?

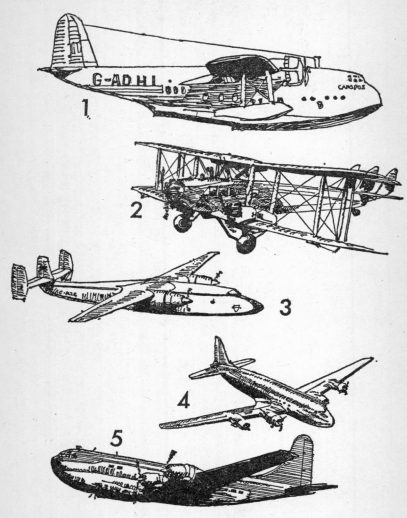

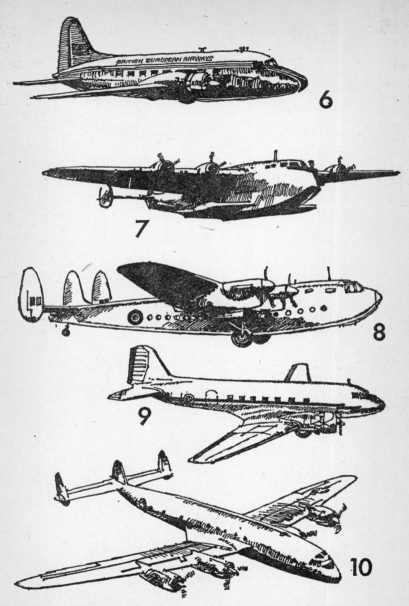

6

7

8

9

10

Passes and tunnels

A In which continental countries are these passes?

1 Grand St Bernard

2 Petit St Bernard

3 Seeberg

4 St Gotthard

5 Brenner

6 Grimsel

7 Simplon

8 Wurzen

9 San Bernardino

B Where are these tunnels?

1 San Bernardino (road)

2 Mont Blanc (road)

3 Grand St Bernard (road)

4 Arlberg (rail)

5 Mont Cenis (rail)

Souvenirs

In which country would you, as a traveller, buy these?

1 A balalaika
2 A pair of moccasins
3 A cuckoo clock
4 Waterford crystal
5 A Wedgwood china tea-set
6 A pot of pâté de foie gras
7 A jar of maple syrup
8 Glass animals
9 A tin of shortbread
10 A Gouda cheese
11 A pair of castanets
12 A boomerang

All at sea

Can you tell what kinds of ships these are?

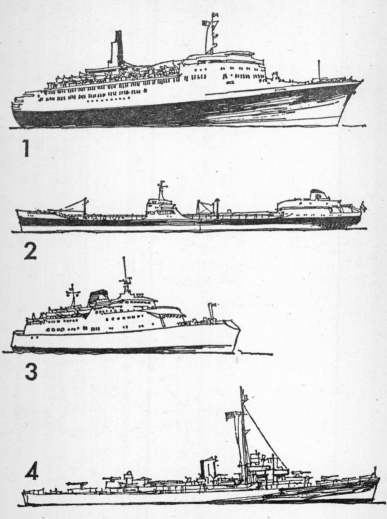

1

2

3

4

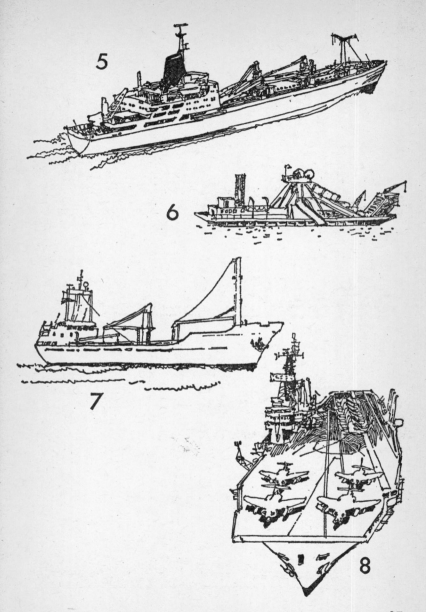

5

6

7

8

Airlines

A To which airlines do these symbols belong?

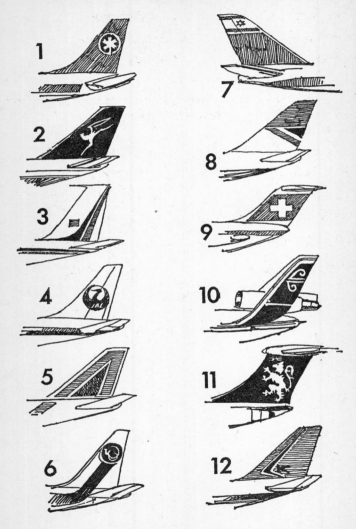

1

2

3

4

5

6

7

8

9

10

11

12

B What is the nationality of these airlines?

1 Sabena
2 Olympic
3 Pan Am
4 Braniff
5 KLM

6 SAS
7 Aer Lingus
8 Aeroflot
9 Lufthansa
10 Iberia

C You can fly on these airlines – but your ticket would show the letters in their *correct* order! Can you unscramble them?

1 STARN DLOWR
2 RAI EFACNR
3 TAQNSA
4 IMPCOYL
5 FAELROOT
6 IAR ADNAAC

7 HUASALFTN
8 RABIEI
9 THISRBI SWAYARI
10 LLATAAII
11 ANP CREAMIAN
12 RAWSSISI

What happened ?

What famous events happened at these places, which are visited by many tourists today, in the years shown?

1 Dunkirk in 1940

2 Waterloo in 1815

3 Paris in 1789

4 Bannockburn in 1314

5 Runnymede in 1215

6 Versailles in 1919

7 Pompeii in AD 79

8 Edgehill in 1642

9 The City of London in 1666

10 Constantinople (now called Istanbul) in 1453

11 Normandy in 1944

12 Whitehall, in London, in 1649

13 Gettysburg in 1863

14 Rouen in 1431

Old crock

Can you see seven ways in which the second picture of this old crock does not match the first?

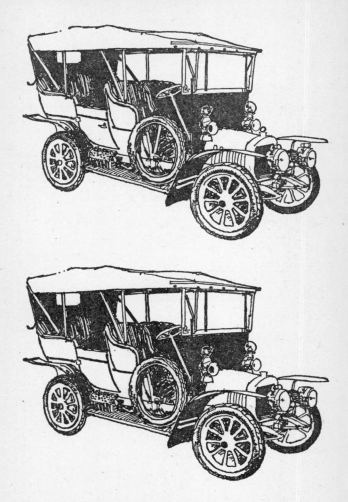

Things you see

Where would you, as a tourist, see these things, and what are they?

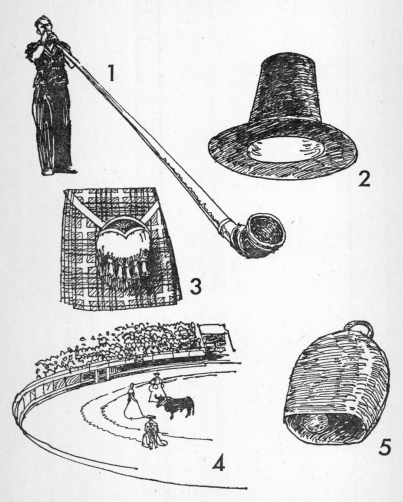

6

7

8

9

10

11

More famous travellers

All these questions are about famous 'travellers'.

1 Where in France did William the Conqueror come from?

2 Nelson sailed from here in *Victory*, and came back here after Trafalgar.

3 Shakespeare left here to travel to London to make his name.

4 Cabot sailed from here in 1497 and went on to discover Newfoundland.

5 Who was Thomas Cook and what was he famous for?

6 'Dr Livingstone, I presume,' said one traveller to another. Who said this, and where did it happen?

7 Which Englishman travelled with a Scotsman on a famous tour of the Hebrides?

8 Who sailed across the Pacific on a balsa raft and what was the name of his famous book about the voyage?

Air words

1 What happens when aircraft are *stacked*?

2 What is an *altimeter*?

3 What is an aircraft's *black box*?

4 Long-distance passengers can have *jet lag*. What does this mean?

5 Why are air passengers asked to *fasten their seat belts*?

6 When do they do this?

7 What happens when a pilot uses *reverse thrust* of the engines?

8 What is a *flight plan*?

9 What is a *boarding pass*?

10 What is an *air lane*?

History can be seen

From the road, track and path you can see living history. What are these and what are the approximate dates when they were built?

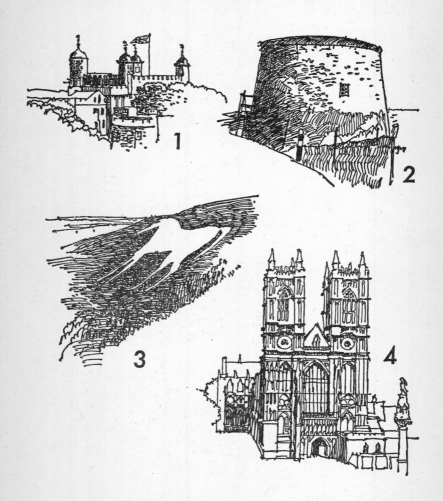

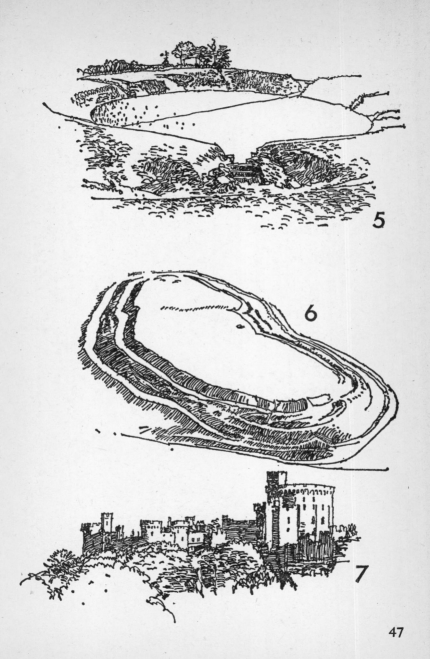

5

6

7

Famous people

All these are famous people. Thousands of tourists visit their graves every year. Where are they buried?

1 Lord Nelson

2 Queen Victoria

3 Napoleon Bonaparte

4 Sir Winston Churchill

5 The Duke of Wellington

6 The Unknown Soldier

7 King George VI

8 President John F. Kennedy

9 William Shakespeare

10 Henry VIII

11 Ludwig van Beethoven

12 General de Gaulle

13 Abraham Lincoln

Tourists' delights

In which countries are these famous attractions for tourists?

1 The Dordogne

2 Snowdonia

3 The Catskill Mountains

4 The Black Forest

5 The Vosges

6 The Cotswolds

7 The Ardennes

8 Campania

9 The Costa Brava

10 The Taunus Mountains

11 The Camargue

12 The Costa del Sol

13 The Dolomites

14 The Riviera

15 The Chilterns

16 The Alps

17 The Algarve

18 The Bernese Oberland

Crazy airport

There are at least 12 mistakes in this picture. How many can you find?

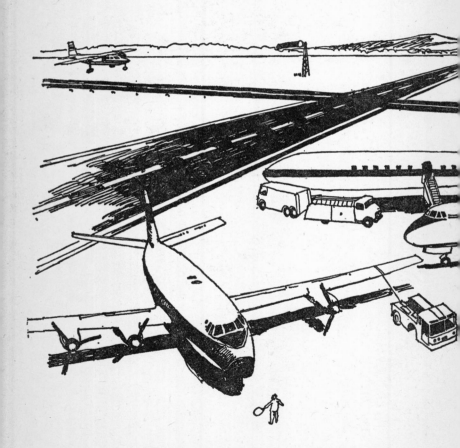

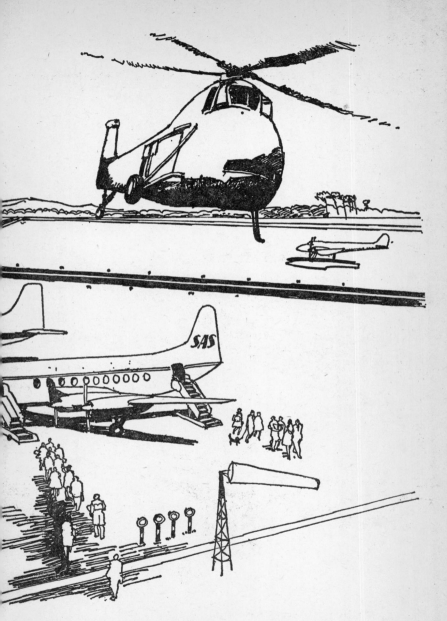

Road signs

What are the meanings of these road signs?

10 11 12

13 14 15

16 17 18

19 20 21

Famous artistic and historic objects

Where can you see these famous artistic and historic objects?

1 The Bayeux Tapestry

2 *The Mona Lisa* by Leonardo da Vinci

3 *The Laughing Cavalier* by Franz Hals

4 The Elgin Marbles

5 *The Last Supper* by Leonardo da Vinci

6 The statue of the Vénus de Milo

7 Charlemagne's Throne

8 The statue of *David* by Michelangelo

9 *Nightwatch* by Rembrandt

10 The Sutton Hoo Treasure

11 The Regalia of Scotland

12 *The Book of Kells*

13 The Rosetta Stone

14 The Obelisk of Luxor

15 Cleopatra's Needle

More true or false ?

Here are nine statements, some of which are true and the others false. Which is which?

1 A dashboard stops stones flying up and hitting a car's windscreen.

2 Citizens of EEC countries can travel within the EEC without obtaining a visa.

3 New York is on the same latitude as Madrid.

4 The shortest air route between London and Los Angeles is over the North Pole.

5 The Arc de Triomphe was built by the British to celebrate their victory over Napoleon at the battle of Waterloo.

6 In 1859 a man called Blondin crossed Niagara Falls on a tightrope.

7 Cleopatra's needle was floated to London from Alexandria in 1877.

8 The Panama Canal was built in 1869 by Ferdinand de Lesseps.

9 Two-thirds of the earth's surface is covered by salt water.

Aircraft silhouettes

These are silhouettes of the airliners on pages 12 and 13.
Can you tell which is which? (They are shown here in a
different order.)

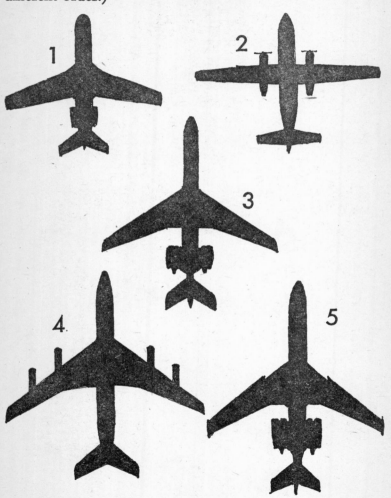

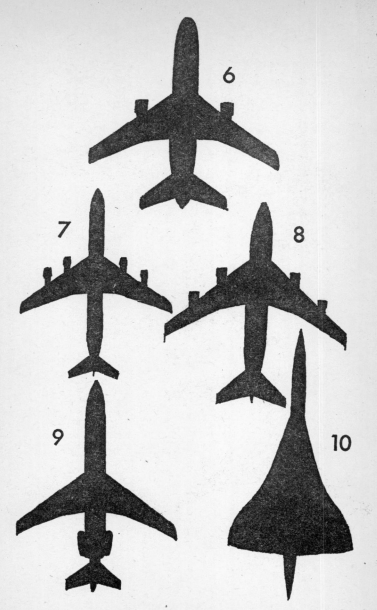

6

7

8

9

10

Motorway questions

1 What is a Motorway?

2 Which Motorway was the first to be opened?

3 Which vehicles are not allowed on a Motorway?

4 What is the maximum speed for a car on a Motorway?

5 What is the main colour of Motorway signs?

6 How far apart are emergency telephones spaced on a Motorway?

7 What do these three exit signs mean?

Foreign Motorway questions

1 In which country today would you drive on:
   (a) An Autobahn
   (b) An Autostrada
   (c) A Turnpike
   (d) An Autoroute

2 Why is (a) better than (b), (c) or (d) for the motorist?

3 What is the Trans-Canada Highway, and where does it begin and end?

4 Where is the Alaska Highway, and where does it start and finish?

5 What was the Burma Road?

6 What was the Via Appia or Appian Way?

7 What is the Cape to Cairo route?

Mountains and volcanoes

What are the names of these? The country is provided as a clue!

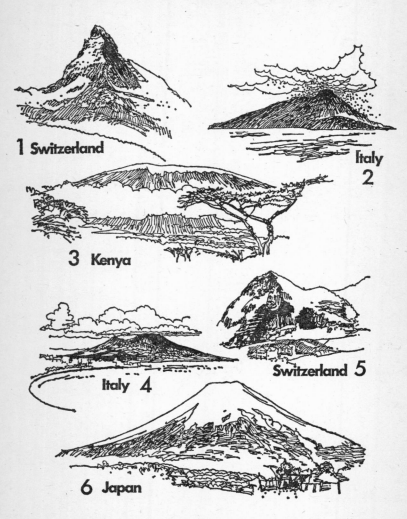

1 Switzerland

Italy 2

3 Kenya

Italy 4

Switzerland 5

6 Japan

Signals at sea

Messages can be sent at sea by radio and lamp signals. For these, Morse Code is often used. Here is the Morse Code.

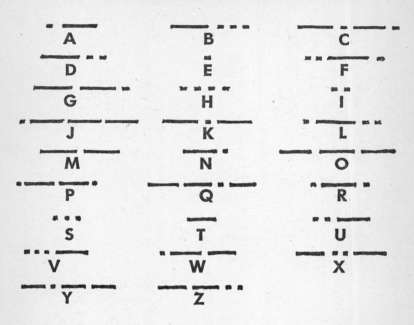

Can you tell what this message is?

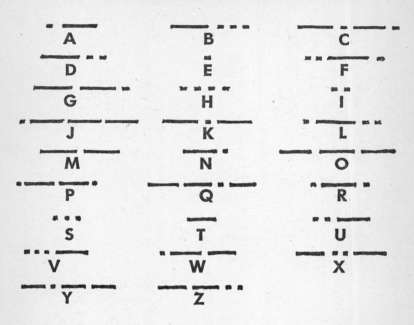

Makes of car

Here are some old and some modern badges of fourteen famous makes of car. Can you identify them?

7

8

9

10

11

12

13

14

Streets and squares

A In which British cities today are these famous streets?

1 Regent Street
2 Princes Street
3 The Shambles
4 The High
5 Petty Cury
6 The Bull Ring
7 Sauchiehall Street
8 Deansgate
9 Broadmead
10 Lime Street

B In which famous foreign cities are these?

1 Champs-Elysées
2 Broadway
3 Unter den Linden
4 O'Connell Street
5 Grand Canal
6 Ringstrasse
7 St Peter's Square
8 Pennsylvania Avenue
9 Red Square
10 Place de la Concorde

At the airport

These can be seen at most airports. What are they?

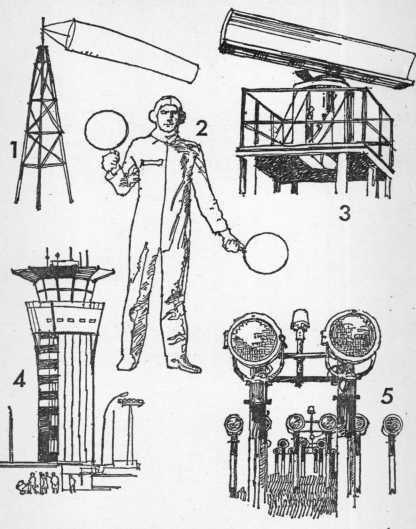

Bridges

Here are some famous road bridges. Which is which?

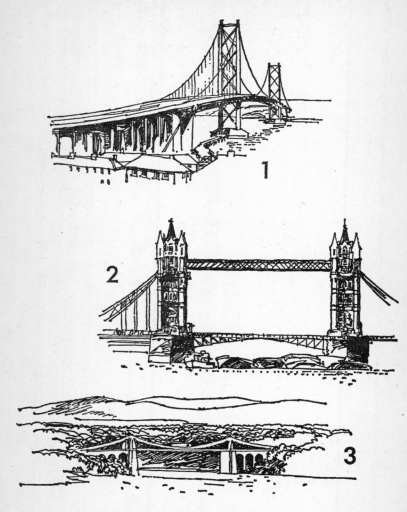

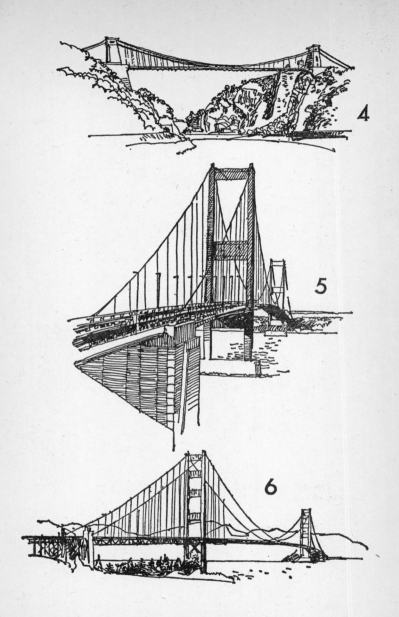

4

5

6

Canals and ferries

A All these are canals for sea-going ships, but where are they?

1 Suez

2 Corinth

3 Manchester

4 Caledonian

5 Erie

6 Panama

7 Kiel

8 St Lawrence Seaway

B Which river or stretch of water do these ferries cross?

1 Woolwich

2 Dartmouth Lower

3 Torpoint

4 Renfrew

5 Ballachulish

6 Portsmouth-Ryde

7 Staten Island

Famous events

What famous events take place in:

1 Siena (Italy) in July and August
2 Calgary (Canada) in July
3 Edinburgh (Scotland) in August
4 Lourdes (France) in February
5 Munich (Germany) in October
6 Llangollen (Wales) in July
7 Nice (France) in February and March
8 Oberammergau (Germany) at Easter once every ten years
9 Monte Carlo in January
10 Bayreuth (Germany) in the summer
11 Wembley (England) in May

Famous pairs

A Can you match one name in the first column with one in the second, and say what each pair was famous for?

1 Alcock		(a)	Livingstone
2 Don Quixote		(b)	Clark
3 Lewis		(c)	Blyth
4 Stanley		(d)	Brown
5 Ridgway		(e)	Sancho Panza

B Can you match each of these famous travellers with his correct 'vehicle'?

1 Hannibal		(a)	*Santa Maria*
2 Chichester		(b)	Camel
3 Stevenson		(c)	*Gipsy Moth*
4 Lawrence		(d)	Huskies
5 Scott		(e)	*Spirit of St Louis*
6 Lindbergh		(f)	Donkey
7 Columbus		(g)	Elephant

On the road

These can be seen on most roads or streets. What are they called?

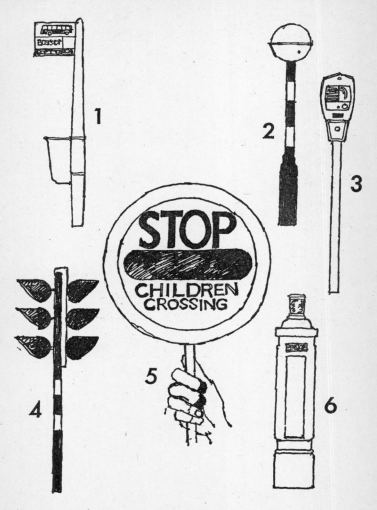

STOP CHILDREN CROSSING

Ports

Here are some famous ports marked by numbers. Can you put correct names to the numbers?

Railway general knowledge

1 What is the Gare du Nord and where is it?

2 Who was George Stephenson and what did he do? Who was Robert Stephenson and what did he do?

3 If you travel by train in the United States you will probably go by Amtrak. What is it and what does it mean?

4 In Britain the man who controls the train is the driver. What is he called in the United States and Canada?

5 What does Motorail mean?

6 Who was, and what is, a Pullman?

7 Who was Isambard Kingdom Brunel and what did he do for railways?

8 Where would you be if you were at Penn Station?

Lakes and islands

A Where are these lakes?

1 Derwentwater

2 Thun

3 Maggiore

4 Lomond

5 Erie

6 Constance

7 Léman

8 Ullswater

9 Como

10 Champlain

B On which lakes are these cities?

1 Chicago

2 Zurich

3 Toronto

4 Detroit

C Where are these islands situated?

1 Mull

2 Newfoundland

3 Isle of Wight

4 Majorca

5 Ascension

6 Sri Lanka

7 Tasmania

8 Corfu

National costume

In which country would you be if you were seeing these ten people?

1

2

3

4

5

6

7

8

9

10

Grand hotels

A As a traveller you would naturally want to stay in the best hotel whenever possible. Which city or town would you be visiting if you had a room in the following hotels?

1 Ritz

2 George V

3 Bernini-Bristol

4 Sacher

5 Frankfurter Hof

6 Dorchester

7 Algonquin

8 North British

B What do the following terms mean in relation to hotels?

1 2-star, 3-star, 4-star, etc.

2 Motel

3 Temperance

4 Tout compris (in France)

5 En pension

6 Paradores

7 A la carte

8 Table d'hôte

Strange railway

This is a strangely run railway, as there are at least ten mistakes in this picture. How many can you spot?

Famous cars

What is the name of each of these famous cars?

6

7

8

9

10

International time

A When it is 12 noon in London (GMT), what time is it in the following places?

1 New York

2 Moscow

3 San Francisco

4 Bombay

5 Paris

6 Teheran

7 Hong Kong

8 Cape Town

9 Sydney

10 Kuala Lumpur

11 Buenos Aires

12 Fiji

B What time is it in London (GMT) when it is 6 pm in the following places?

1 Manila

2 Vancouver

3 Oslo

4 Cairo

5 Chicago

6 Athens

7 Nairobi

8 Colombo

Air knowledge

1 Which is the 'odd plane out' in each of these groups of aircraft? (The answers have nothing to do with the names.)
   (a) Vickers VC10, Boeing 747, BAC 1-11, Douglas DC8
   (b) De Havilland Comet 4, BAC Vanguard, Boeing 727, Lockheed Tristar

2 IATA is an important set of initials in air travel. What do they mean, and what does IATA do?

3 Can you name at least ten British cities or towns with airports used by airlines.

4 Airlines fix special labels to your luggage to show the city you are flying to. They have an international code system (it's not a secret one!) and here are some: LAX, LON, SYD, ANK, PAR, JNB, BUE, GLA, MOW, BOM, WAW, NBO. If they were on your luggage where would you be going to?

5 Who was the Briton who designed the first jet engine?

6 What is the name of the fuel used in jet engines?

7 How many miles non-stop from:
   (a) London to New York
   (b) Paris to Rome
   (c) Cairo to Nairobi
   (d) Sydney to Wellington
   (e) Bombay to Tokyo
   (f) Buenos Aires to Madrid
   (g) San Francisco to Honolulu

Railway signals and signs

Many travellers know the meaning of these as well as the drivers do. How many do you know?

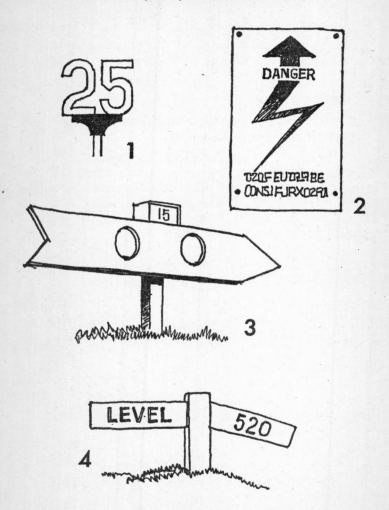

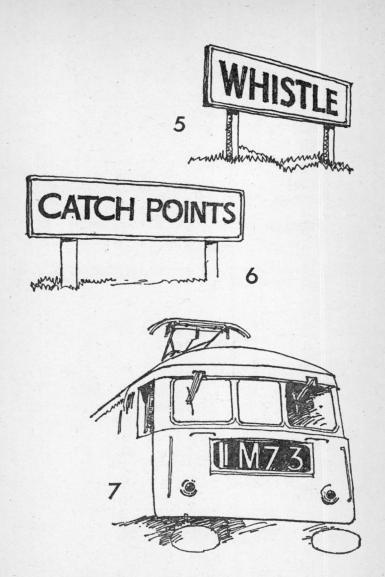

5

6

7

Knowing London

Do you know your way around London? See if you can answer these questions.

1 In which famous road is Buckingham Palace?

2 Which particular station would you use to go to (a) Brighton, (b) Dover, (c) Winchester, (d) Norwich, (e) Liverpool, (f) Birmingham, (g) Edinburgh, (h) Plymouth?

3 What is a Red Rover ticket, and how useful is it?

4 Between which two bridges are the Houses of Parliament situated?

5 Which museums are in South Kensington?

6 In which park is London Zoo?

7 Which are the four most famous shopping streets in the West End?

8 Which bridge is nearest to the sea?

9 How tall is the Post Office Tower and what is its main use?

10 Which are the two famous cricket grounds in London?

11 Which house, now an interesting museum, was called 'Number one, London' when a very famous man lived in it?

12 Where is the Chamber of Horrors?

13 This question is perhaps much harder to answer than the others. Where does Charles I look across the road at Oliver Cromwell?

Famous arches

Where are these famous arches, and what are their names?

1

2

3

4

5

Motoring safety

Do you know what the Highway Code is? These questions are all based on the Highway Code.

1 What are the colours of traffic lights?

2 In what order do they appear?

3 Some traffic lights have a green arrow signal. What does this signal mean?

4 Why must drivers take special care near a parked ice-cream van?

5 If your car approaches a red reflecting triangle placed on the road, what must the driver be ready for?

6 A cyclist must pay attention to the care of his or her bicycle, but four things in particular must be in good condition. What are they?

7 When approaching a roundabout does a driver give way to traffic coming from the right?

8 When you want to walk across the road, what must you do at the kerb?

9 When and why should a driver and passenger wear seat belts?

10 What must a motor cyclist always wear?

Navigation help

Ships have to be navigated in and out of harbour, when special aids are used to help the captain or the pilot. See if you recognise these.

Parts of vehicles

These are parts of vehicles which you may have seen as a traveller. Can you name the whole vehicle?

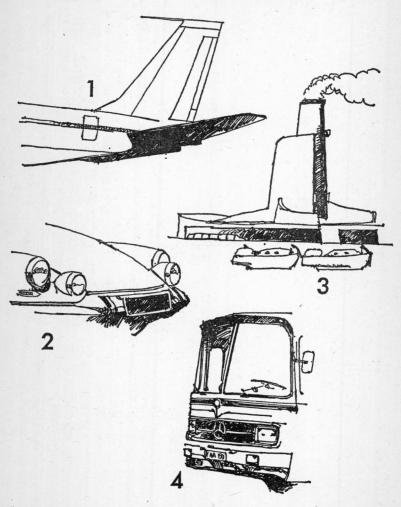

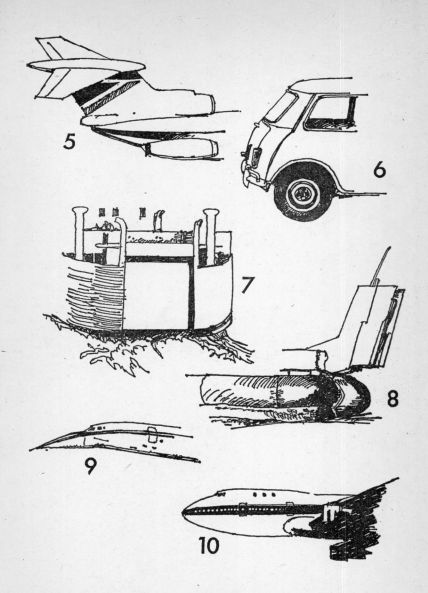

5

6

7

8

9

10

Oceans and seas

A What ocean or sea would you cross to go from:

1 Dover to Calais

2 Naples to Algiers

3 Mombasa to Bombay

4 Suez to Aden

5 Hamburg to Stockholm

6 New York to Southampton

7 San Francisco to Wellington

8 Tokyo to Shanghai

9 Istanbul to Sebastopol?

B Can you name three inland seas?

C Where are these Straits?

1 Magellan

2 Johore

3 Menai

4 Bass

5 Bering

6 Gibraltar

Road travel

1 If you were a traveller on the historic Appian Way, where would you be, and what kind of wheeled traffic would you meet?

2 Where is
   (a) The Road to the Isles
   (b) The Road to Samarkand?

3 What famous race takes place on the Brighton Road?

4 In which Dickens novel did a traveller use the Dover Road?

5 What was a 'Gentleman of the Road'?

6 From which spot in London are road distances from London measured?

7 What do Stane Street, Watling Street and Ermine Street have in common?

8 Name two famous British road engineers.

9 What was a turnpike?

10 'All roads lead to ———.' Where?

11 What is
   (a) A road-hog
   (b) A road-runner
   (c) A road-roller?

World capitals

Each number on the map represents a city. Can you name them?

Answers

Great sights

1 Leaning Tower of Pisa, Italy. 2 Taj Mahal, Agra, India. 3 Eiffel Tower, Paris, France. 4 St Paul's Cathedral, London. 5 Pyramids of Gizeh, Egypt. 6 Statue of Liberty, New York, USA. 7 Table Mountain, Capetown, South Africa. 8 Sydney Harbour Bridge, Australia. 9 Parthenon, Athens, Greece. 10 Colosseum, Rome, Italy. 11 Great Wall of China. 12 Sugar Loaf Mountain, Rio de Janeiro, Brazil.

10 **Travel words**

1 A passport is a document issued by a government to a citizen which authorises him or her to travel abroad and which guarantees the person the protection of the government. 2 A special cheque, bought at a bank, which only the buyer can cash at a hotel, shop or another bank at home or abroad. It is safer than carrying actual money. 3 When a ship crosses the Equator (the 'Line') a ceremony is held for the passengers who have not crossed the Equator before; amusing and harmless things are done to them, such as shaving them with a big wooden razor. They are given a certificate. 4 Immigration is the movement of people into a country in order to live there permanently. The Immigration Department controls the entry of foreigners.

5 Quarantine precautions are taken if a ship, aircraft or traveller is suspected of carrying a dangerous disease. Many animals entering Britain must go into quarantine, such as special kennels, for six months. 6 Lifeboat drill is a regular drill for the passengers and crew of a ship and it accustoms them to the number and position of the lifeboat they would go to in an emergency. 7 Crossing the bar means crossing the entrance of a harbour. 8 A visa is an extra document which a traveller has to obtain to visit some countries. It is often a special stamp on your passport. 9 Special taxes on certain goods are called customs duties. A customs officer is an official who checks your baggage when you move from one country to another. Douane is the French word for customs, and is used internationally. 10 Time has to be measured from a particular meridian and this was established in 1884 as the Greenwich Standard meridian (0° longitude). GMT stands for Greenwich Mean Time, which is now called British Standard Time. 11 The International Date Line is the 180th meridian, which divides eastern time from western time; you 'gain' a day when you cross it when going westwards and you 'lose' a day when going eastwards. 12 Travel sickness can afflict travellers in a variety of ways, such as air, car or sea sickness. It can be brought on by worry, by losing balance, by bumps and jerks, or by other causes. 13 If you are travelling you can have letters sent poste restante, i.e., sent to a particular post

office to be collected by you. **14** The Equator is the imaginary line which encircles the earth, is midway between the North and South Poles, and divides it into the Northern and Southern hemispheres. **15** Latitude is the distance, measured in degrees, minutes and seconds, of a point north or south of the Equator. The Equator is 0° latitude. **16** Longitude is the distance, measured in degrees, minutes and seconds, of a point east or west of the Standard meridian at Greenwich, England. This meridian is 0° longitude. **17** Mayday is the international radio call sign for a ship or aeroplane in distress. **18** A port health authority is the department of a seaport or airport which enforces the laws concerned with health and disease, such as the smallpox and rabies regulations.

11   **True or False?**

1 False. A US gallon is equivalent to about 6½ Imperial pints, approximately three-quarters of an Imperial gallon. **2** False. Chopsticks are used in China. **3** True. **4** False. Dogs and cats and various other animals must go into quarantine. **5** True. It has been sinking very slowly for many years. **6** True. Babies under two are carried free on some routes. **7** True. Nineteenth-century railwaymen used a red neckerchief for waving in an emergency. **8** False. The nautical mile is 6080 feet and the statute mile is 5280 feet. **9** True. James Watt devised the unit of power after tests on strong dray horses. 10 False. The name is that of a public house.

12/13 Airliners

1 Boeing 707. 2 Hawker Siddeley Trident Three. 3 Douglas DC-8. 4 Caravelle. 5 Lockheed Tristar. 6 Boeing 747. 7 Fokker Friendship. 8 Vickers VC10. 9 Concorde. 10 Ilyushin Il-62 'Classic'.

14 Famous stations and famous trains

A 1 Bristol. 2 London. 3 Liverpool. 4 Leeds. 5 London. 6 Edinburgh. 7 Exeter. 8 Manchester. 9 Bradford and Liverpool. 10 Bath. 11 Glasgow. 12 Birmingham. B 1 Paris and Bucharest. 2 London and Edinburgh. 3 London and Penzance. 4 Paris and the South of France at night. There is also a South African Blue Train which runs from Johannesburg to Capetown. 5 London and Bristol. 6 Chicago and Los Angeles. 7 Paris and Nice. 8 The Hook of Holland and Basle. 9 London and Sheffield. 10 London and Norwich.

15 Crazy map

1 Aberdeen. 2 Dunbar. 3 Scarborough. 4 Filey. 5 Yarmouth. 6 Margate. 7 Eastbourne. 8 Brighton. 9 Southsea. 10 Bournemouth. 11 Torquay. 12 Newquay. 13 Ilfracombe. 14 Aberystwyth. 15 Rhyl. 16 Blackpool. 17 Morecambe.

16   **Capital fun**

A 1 Paris. 2 Madrid. 3 Cairo. 4 Washington DC.
5 London. 6 Canberra. 7 Lagos. 8 Dublin. 9 Stockholm. 10 Berne. 11 Moscow. 12 Delhi. B 1 South
Africa. 2 Norway. 3 Belgium. 4 Italy. 5 Turkey.
6 Portugal. 7 Algeria. 8 Kenya. 9 Japan. 10 Austria.
11 The Netherlands. 12 Czechoslovakia.

17   **Puzzle cars**

1 Ford. 2 Jaguar. 3 Volvo. 4 Chrysler. 5 Vauxhall.
6 Rover. 7 Morris. 8 Citroen. 9 Mercedes.
10 Renault. 11 Fiat. 12 Volkswagen.

18   **Uniforms around the world**

1 Greece (Evzone). 2 Canada (Mountie). 3 Britain
(Lifeguard). 4 The Vatican (Papal Guard). 5 France
(Gendarme). 6 Spain (Civil Guard). 7 Britain
(Scottish piper).

19   **Odd loco**

The fourth locomotive; the driver's side window
has no division.

20   **Money around the world**

1 France and Switzerland. 2 Japan. 3 Spain.

4 Germany. 5 The Netherlands. 6 USA, Canada, Australia, Hong Kong, Singapore, New Zealand, British Honduras. 7 South Africa. 8 Austria. 9 Britain, Irish Republic. 10 Greece. 11 Yugoslavia, Tunisia, Iraq, Algeria, Jordan, Kuwait. 12 Sweden, Iceland. 13 Italy. 14 Portugal. 15 Finland. 16 India, Pakistan. 17 USSR. 18 Denmark, Norway.

21 **Famous travellers – real and fictional**

1 (a) *Around the World in Eighty Days*, (b) Phileas Fogg and Passepartout, (c) Charing Cross Station, London, (d) Horse-cab, train, steamship, elephant, horse-carriage, schooner, paddle-steamer, sledge. 2 Dick Whittington, who was to become Sir Richard Whittington, and Lord Mayor of London three times. 3 Marco Polo. 4 The Americans Neil Armstrong and Edwin Aldrin on 20th July, 1969. 5 Agatha Christie. 6 A Frenchman, Louis Blériot, in 1909. 7 Dr Crippen. 8 Robert Louis Stevenson.

22 **Airports**

1 Paris. 2 Athens. 3 New York. 4 Amsterdam. 5 Colombo. 6 Berlin. 7 London. 8 Tokyo. 9 Chicago. 10 Geneva. 11 Rome. 12 Montreal. 13 Singapore. 14 Sydney. 15 Lagos. 16 Bombay. 17 Teheran. 18 Calcutta. 19 Capetown. 20 Tel Aviv.

23   Odd vehicles

1 Hovercraft. 2 Rickshaw. 3 Ski-lift. 4 Gondola.
5 Bobsleigh. 6 Hot-air balloon.

24   Railway words

1 The fast passenger trains which travel between
the main cities of Britain. 2 An express goods train.
3 The *up line* is the line on which London-bound
trains travel; the *down line* is the opposite of this.
4 It is the distance between the rails, i.e., 4 feet
8½ inches. 5 The numbers and letters on the front
of a locomotive. 6 A system of braking for the
whole train, operated by the driver; until fairly
recently goods trucks could not be braked by the
driver. 7 A season ticket can last for a week, month,
quarter or year; a cheap day ticket costs less than an
ordinary return ticket, but usually you must start
your journey after the rush hour. 8 A level-crossing
which does not have a keeper. 9 This is a particular
train's right to proceed when the green signal
shows. 10 Southern Railway; London and North
Eastern Railway; Great Western Railway; London
Midland and Scottish Railway.

25   Motoring words

A 1 Brakes which work by pads pressing on a disc
behind the wheel. 2 Cogs which help to transmit

the power from the engine to the wheels. 3 An instrument, usually a dial or a strip, which tells the driver the speed of the car, and records the mileage. 4 A special high gear. 5 One of the chambers of the engine in which the fuel is burned. 6 The device at the top of the cylinder which ignites the fuel. 7 The device which mixes air with petrol vapour for burning in the cylinders. 8 An engine has to be turned over in order to start; a starter is a small, powerful electric motor which does this. 9 The distributor conveys electric current to the sparking plugs so that they fire in the right order. 10 A device which generates electricity for the car. 11 A meter which indicates the electric current flow into and out of the battery. 12 Gears which allow for different road speeds of the driving wheels.
B 1 The government licence which allows a vehicle to be driven on public roads. 2 The two main forms of tyre. 3 A motoring or driving competition. 4 A device for lifting a wheel or side of a car. 5 A tunnel under another road. 6 A fault in the steering which causes the car to go slightly wide at corners. 7 The edge of a Motorway on which cars are allowed to stop in an emergency. 8 The official time for switching on lights. 9 Italian for grand touring: it describes luxury motoring with high performance. 10 An international document which shows the driver is insured for foreign travel.

26/27   Famous sights

1 Stonehenge. 2 Tower Bridge. 3 Hadrian's Wall.
4 Salisbury Cathedral. 5 Caernarvon Castle. 6 Nelson's Column. 7 Silbury Hill. 8 Post Office Tower.
9 Giant's Causeway. 10 Edinburgh Castle.

28   Food around the world

A 1 USA. 2 Switzerland. 3 England. 4 Austria.
5 France. 6 China. 7 Italy. 8 Austria. 9 Greece.
10 Scandinavia. 11 Germany. 12 India. 13 France.
14 China. B 1 Italy. 2 England. 3 The Netherlands.
4 France. 5 Scotland. 6 Scotland. 7 Switzerland.
8 Greece. 9 Italy. 10 France.

29   Odd car out

The fifth car; one light is missing.

30   In a foreign language

A 1 Spanish. 2 Dutch. 3 Italian. 4 Russian.
5 French. 6 Swedish. 7 Portuguese. 8 German.
B 1 Yes: French. 2 Yes: German, Dutch, Swedish.
3 Yes: Italian, Spanish. 4 No: Russian. 5 No:
French. 6 If you please: French. 7 Please: Italian.
8 Please: German. 9 Men and women: French.
10 Women and men: German. (Both 9 and 10 are
the signs for lavatories.)

31   **Motoring initials**

A 1 Automobile Association (Britain). 2 Royal
Automobile Club (Britain). 3 Touring Club de
France. 4 Allgemeiner Deutscher Automobil-Club
(West Germany). 5 Touring Club Suisse (Switzerland). 6 Real Autômovil Club de España (Spain).
7 Österreichischer   Automobil-Motorrad-und-
Touring-Club (Austria). 8 Touring Club Italiano
(Italy). B 1 Norway. 2 Netherlands. 3 France.
4 Greece. 5 Germany. 6 Great Britain. 7 Canada.
8 Luxembourg. 9 Malta. 10 Yugoslavia. C 1 B.
2 S. 3 CH. 4 H. 5 USA. 6 I. 7 GBJ. 8 E. 9 SF. 10 P.

32/33 **Vintage airliners**

1 Short Empire 'C' class. 2 De Havilland DH66
Hercules. 3 Elizabethan. 4 Douglas DC-4. 5 Boeing
Stratocruiser. 6 Vickers Viking. 7 Boeing Clipper.
8 Avro York. 9 Douglas DC-3 Dakota. 10 Lockheed Constellation.

34   **Passes and tunnels**

A 1 Switzerland–Italy. 2 France–Italy. 3 Austria–
Yugoslavia.   4 Switzerland.   5 Austria–Italy.
6 Switzerland. 7 Switzerland–Italy. 8 Austria–
Yugoslavia. 9 Switzerland. B 1 Switzerland.
2 France–Italy. 3 Switzerland–Italy. 4 Austria.
5 France–Italy.

35   **Souvenirs**

   1 Russia. 2 Canada, USA. 3 Switzerland, Germany.
   4 Irish Republic. 5 England. 6 France. 7 Canada.
   8 Italy. 9 Scotland. 10 Netherlands. 11 Spain.
   12 Australia.

36/37 **All at sea**

   1 Passenger liner. 2 Tanker. 3 Cross-channel ferry.
   4 Frigate. 5 Container ship. 6 Dredger. 7 Freighter.
   8 Aircraft carrier.

38/39 **Airlines**

   A 1 Air Canada. 2 Qantas. 3 China Airlines.
   4 Japan Airlines. 5 Alitalia. 6 Air Jamaica. 7 El Al.
   8 British Airways. 9 Swissair. 10 Air New Zealand.
   11 British Caledonian. 12 South African Airways.
   B 1 Belgium. 2 Greece. 3 USA. 4 USA. 5 Netherlands. 6 Scandinavia. 7 Irish Republic. 8 USSR.
   9 West Germany. 10 Spain. C 1 Trans World. 2 Air
   France. 3 Qantas. 4 Olympic. 5 Aeroflot. 6 Air
   Canada. 7 Lufthansa. 8 Iberia. 9 British Airways.
   10 Alitalia. 11 Pan American. 12 Swissair.

40   **What happened?**

   1 Evacuation of the British Army. 2 Defeat of
   Napoleon. 3 Fall of the Bastille. 4 English defeated

by the Scots under Robert the Bruce. **5** Signing of the Magna Carta by King John. **6** Treaty of Versailles signed by the Allies and Germany. **7** Vesuvius erupted and completely covered the city of Pompeii. **8** The first battle of the English Civil War. **9** The Great Fire. **10** It was captured by the Turks. **11** The Allied invasion of Western Europe. **12** Charles I was beheaded. **13** Battle of the American Civil War, won by the North; it was the turning point of the War. **14** Joan of Arc was burned there.

41   Old crock

1 Part of nearside hood support is missing. **2** Radiator cap is missing. **3** Top of nearside headlamp is missing. **4** Spoke of nearside front wheel is missing. **5** Offside bonnet air vents are missing. **6** Offside door handle is missing. **7** Brake handle is missing.

42/43   Things you see

1 Alpenhorn: Switzerland, Austria. **2** Welsh hat: Wales. **3** Kilt: Scotland. **4** Bull ring: Spain, France, Portugal, Mexico. **5** Cow bell: Switzerland, Austria. **6** Lederhosen: Germany. **7** Clogs: Netherlands. **8** Wine flask: Spain. **9** Tarboosh: Egypt, Morocco, Algeria, Tunisia. **10** Hookah or water pipe: China, Malaysia, Singapore, Hong Kong. **11** Beer stein: Germany, Austria.

44   More famous travellers

1 Falaise, in Normandy. 2 Portsmouth. 3 Stratford-on-Avon. 4 Bristol. 5 Lived 1808–1892, organised the first train excursion, became the first commercial travel agent for tours at home and abroad, published travel guides. 6 Sir Henry Morton Stanley, 1841–1904, who found Dr Livingstone near Lake Tanganyika in 1871. 7 The Englishman Dr Samuel Johnson travelled with the Scotsman James Boswell on a tour of the Hebrides in 1773. 8 Thor Heyerdahl; *The Kon-Tiki Expedition*.

45   Air words

1 They fly above each other, over certain points, while waiting to land. 2 A meter which indicates a plane's height. 3 An indestructible instrument which can be examined to find out what went wrong if the aircraft were to crash. 4 The temporary changes in a person's senses when he moves from one time zone to another. 5 So that they will not be thrown about and become injured if the aircraft lurches or jerks violently. 6 On take-off, on landing and when there is bad flying weather. Nowadays, many aircraft captains advise passengers to keep their seat belts fastened all the time except when they want to leave their seats. 7 He reverses the flow of the engine in order to produce a braking effect on landing. 8 The programme and instructions,

such as route, height and speed, which the pilot will follow on his flight. **9** A card, issued to you when you book in at the airport, which shows details of how and when you are to board the aircraft and which gate to use. Sometimes it shows your seat number. **10** A recognised air route across a territory.

46/47 **History can be seen**

1 The White Tower, 1078, in the Tower of London. **2** A martello tower, 1804, to be seen on the southeast coast of Britain. **3** The White Horse, Westbury, Wiltshire; cut in the chalk in 1873 on the site of an earlier figure. **4** Westminster Abbey, built in the thirteenth to fifteenth centuries. **5** The Roman amphitheatre, Caerleon, Gwent. **6** Maiden Castle, Dorset; prehistoric. **7** Windsor Castle, founded by William the Conqueror.

48 **Famous people**

1 St Paul's Cathedral, London. **2** Frogmore, Windsor. **3** Hôtel des Invalides, Paris. **4** Bladon churchyard, Oxfordshire. **5** St Paul's Cathedral, London. **6** Westminster Abbey, London. **7** St George's Chapel, Windsor. **8** Arlington Cemetery, Virginia. **9** Stratford-on-Avon, Warwickshire. **10** St George's Chapel, Windsor. **11** Central Cemetery, Vienna. **12** Colombey les deux Eglises, France. **13** Oak Ridge Cemetery, Springfield, Illinois.

49 Tourists' delights

1 France. 2 Wales. 3 USA. 4 West Germany.
5 France. 6 England. 7 France, Belgium, Luxembourg. 8 Italy. 9 Spain. 10 West Germany.
11 France. 12 Spain. 13 Italy. 14 France and Italy.
15 England. 16 Italy, France, Switzerland, Germany,
Liechtenstein and Austria. 17 Portugal. 18 Switzerland.

50/51 Crazy airport

1 Helicopter: one wheel missing, tail rotor missing.
2 The seaplane is landing on the runway. 3 The
light aircraft is landing in the opposite direction on
the same runway. 4 The windsocks are blowing in
opposite directions. 5 Furthest aircraft: wings
missing, cockpit windows missing. 6 Left-hand
aircraft: one engine missing, one propeller blade
missing. 7 Fuel tanker: front wheels missing; fuel
hoses run to the wing of the aircraft. 8 Right-hand
aircraft: tail plane missing; steps missing on forward stairs. 9 The landing lights in the foreground
should not be there.

52/53 Road signs

1 Roundabout ahead. 2 Maximum speed limit
30 mph. 3 Children ahead. 4 Traffic signals
ahead. 5 Cattle on road. 6 Distance to stop sign

ahead. 7 Double bend, first to left (may be reversed).
8 Cross roads ahead. 9 Indicates danger ahead; a
plate below the sign may specify. 10 No entry.
11 Pedestrian crossing ahead. 12 Ahead only.
13 Bend to right (may be reversed). 14 T-junction
ahead. 15 Level crossing with other barrier or gate
ahead. 16 Hump-backed bridge. 17 Maximum
speed limit 70, 60 or 50 mph according to the road.
18 Steep hill upwards. 19 No right turn. 20 Road
narrows. 21 Quayside or river bank ahead.

54   **Famous artistic and historic objects**

1 Bayeux Museum, France. 2 The Louvre, Paris.
3 Wallace Collection, London. 4 British Museum,
London. 5 Church of Santa Maria delle Grazie,
Milan. 6 The Louvre, Paris. 7 The Palatine Chapel,
Aachen. 8 The Galleria dell' Accadamia, Florence.
9 The Rijksmuseum, Amsterdam. 10 British
Museum, London. 11 Edinburgh Castle. 12 Trinity
College, Dublin. 13 British Museum, London.
14 Place de la Concorde, Paris. 15 The Embank-
ment, London.

55   **More true or false?**

1 False. A dashboard is the instrument panel.
2 True. 3 True. 4 True. 5 False. Napoleon started
the building of it to celebrate his victories of 1805–
1806. 6 True. He repeated his achievement a

number of times. **7** True. Its partner was erected in Central Park, New York. **8** False. It was the Suez Canal. The Panama Canal was first used by ships in 1914 but was formally opened in 1920. **9** True.

56/57 **Aircraft silhouettes**

1 Caravelle. **2** Fokker Friendship. **3** Vickers VC 10. **4** Boeing 707. **5** Ilyushin Il-62 'Classic'. **6** Lockheed Tristar. **7** Douglas DC-8. **8** Boeing 747. **9** Hawker Siddeley Trident Three. **10** Concorde.

58 **Motorway questions**

1 A wide road, divided by a central reservation, with two or three lanes in each direction, for high speed driving; it has limited access. **2** The southern section of the M1 opened in 1959. **3** Learner drivers, pedal cycles, motor cycles under 50 cc capacity, some invalid carriages, some slow moving vehicles, agricultural vehicles and animals. **4** 70 mph. **5** Blue, with white lettering. **6** Approximately 1 mile. **7** They are 'count-down' markers at the exits, and each bar represents 100 yards to the exit.

59 **Foreign motorway questions**

1 (a) Germany, (b) Italy, (c) USA, (d) France. **2** Because a motorist does not pay on any of the autobahns. **3** It is a major road which crosses Canada from the Atlantic to the Pacific; from St John's, Newfoundland to Victoria, British Columbia. **4** It is 1523 miles in length, runs from Dawson Creek, British Columbia to Fairbanks, Alaska, and is part of the Pan-American Highway. **5** The road from Lashio, Burma to Chungking, China in the Second World War. **6** The famous Roman road from Brindisi to Rome, along which St Paul travelled to Rome. **7** The road, often just a track, from Cairo in Egypt to Capetown in South Africa. Car races have taken place on it in the past.

60 **Mountains and volcanoes**

1 The Matterhorn. **2** Stromboli. **3** Kilimanjaro. **4** Vesuvius. **5** The Eiger. **6** Fujiyama.

61 **Signals at sea**

The message reads: You are reading a quiz book.

62/63 **Makes of car**

1 Mercedes. **2** Citroen. **3** Austin. **4** Maserati. **5** Alfa Romeo. **6** Morris. **7** Volkswagen. **8** Volvo. **9** Vauxhall. **10** Triumph. **11** Rover. **12** Renault. **13** Opel. **14** Jaguar.

64　**Streets and squares**

A 1 London.　2 Edinburgh.　3 York.　4 Oxford.
5 Cambridge.　6 Birmingham.　7 Glasgow.
8 Manchester. 9 Bristol. 10 Liverpool. **B** 1 Paris.
2 New York.　3 Berlin.　4 Dublin.　5 Venice.
6 Vienna. 7 Rome. 8 Washington DC. 9 Moscow.
10 Paris.

65　**At the airport**

1 Windsock. 2 Marshaller; he guides aircraft on the
apron. 3 Radar scanner. 4 Control tower. 5 Landing
approach lights.

66/67　**Bridges**

1 Forth Road Bridge, Scotland. 2 Tower Bridge,
London.　3 Menai Suspension Bridge, Wales.
4 Clifton Bridge, Bristol.　5 Severn Bridge.
6 Golden Gate, San Francisco.

68　**Canals and ferries**

A 1 Egypt. 2 Greece. 3 England. 4 Scotland. 5
USA. 6 The Panama Canal Zone. 7 West Germany.
8 Canada and USA. **B** 1 Thames. 2 Dart. 3 Tamar
Estuary. 4 Clyde. 5 Loch Leven. 6 Spithead. 7 New
York Harbour.

Famous events

1 Corsa del Palio. 2 The Stampede. 3 The Festival.
4 The Festival of St Bernadette. 5 The Oktoberfest.
6 The International Eisteddfod. 7 The Battle of the
Flowers carnival. 8 The Passion play. 9 Motor car
rally. 10 The Wagner festival. 11 The Football
Association Cup-final match.

Famous pairs

A 1 Alcock and Brown were the first men to fly the
Atlantic. 2 Don Quixote and Sancho Panza were
the two main characters in Cervantes' novel *Don
Quixote*. 3 Lewis and Clark were famous US
explorers in the far West in 1804–1806. 4 Stanley
and Livingstone were nineteenth-century explorers
of Africa. 5 Ridgway and Blyth rowed across the
Atlantic in 1966. **B** 1 Hannibal was a Carthaginian
general who used elephants in his campaign against
Rome in 218 BC. 2 *Gipsy Moth* was the name of a
series of sailing boats used by Sir Francis Chi-
chester in his solo expeditions, e.g., in 1966–7
when he sailed round the world in *Gipsy Moth IV*.
3 Stevenson travelled with a donkey – see page 21
question 8. 4 T. E. Lawrence used camels in his
desert campaigns in the 1914–18 war. 5 Scott was
the leader of the Antarctic expeditions in 1901–1904
and 1910–1912, which used huskies and sledges.
6 Lindbergh made the first non-stop solo flight

across the Atlantic in the plane the *Spirit of St Louis* in 1927. 7 In 1492 Columbus discovered America. The *Santa Maria* was his flagship.

71   **On the road**

1 Bus stop. 2 Belisha beacon, used to indicate a pedestrian crossing. 3 Parking meter. 4 Traffic lights. 5 Sign used by a school crossing patrol to halt traffic (lollipop lady). 6 Police box.

72/73   **Ports**

1 Aberdeen. 2 Belfast. 3 Liverpool. 4 Hull. 5 London. 6 Southampton. 7 Dover. 8 Cherbourg. 9 Dieppe. 10 Boulogne. 11 Calais. 12 Ostend. 13 Zeebrugge. 14 Antwerp. 15 Amsterdam. 16 Hamburg. 17 Copenhagen. 18 Malmö. 19 Göteborg. 20 Oslo. 21 Stockholm.

74   **Railway general knowledge**

1 A railway station in Paris. 2 George Stephenson (1781–1848) was one of the first and greatest railway engineers and built the *Rocket*. His son Robert (1803–59) was almost as well-known as a civil engineer and built many famous bridges which are still in use. 3 Amtrak is the name of the reorganised and partly nationalised American railway system. A few of the old companies remain also. The word

stands for 'American trackage'. **4** The engineer. **5** It is the British Rail long-distance service for carrying cars, drivers and passengers on special trucks. **6** George Mortimer Pullman (1831–97) was an American inventor who organised luxury dining and sleeping railway coaches. The idea later spread to Britain. **7** I. K. Brunel (1806–59) was the engineer of the Great Western Railway, built many fine bridges which are still in use, and designed many of the first steamships. His *Great Britain* (1843) is now on show in Bristol. **8** Penn Station is in New York.

75   **Lakes and islands**

A 1 England. **2** Switzerland. **3** Italy. **4** Scotland. **5** Canada and USA. **6** Germany, Austria and Switzerland. **7** Switzerland and France. **8** England. **9** Italy. **10** USA. **B 1** Lake Michigan. **2** Lake Zurich. **3** Lake Ontario. **4** Lake Erie. **C 1** Inner Hebrides. **2** East coast of Canada. **3** South coast of England. **4** Western Mediterranean. **5** South Atlantic. **6** Indian Ocean. **7** South of the Australian mainland. **8** Ionian Sea.

76/77   **National costume**

1 Switzerland. **2** Netherlands. **3** Japan. **4** Mexico. **5** Wales. **6** Russia. **7** Germany. **8** Spain. **9** Arabia. **10** China.

78   **Grand hotels**

A 1 London. 2 Paris. 3 Rome. 4 Vienna. 5 Frank-
furt. 6 London. 7 New York. 8 Edinburgh. **B** 1 The
number of stars usually refers to the type of hotel
(its number of rooms, private bathrooms and
suites, restaurants, etc.) and not its merit. 2 A hotel
catering specially for motorists. 3 One which does
not serve any alcoholic drinks. 4 Everything
included – i.e., service. 5 The phrase used when
indicating the cost of the bedroom and all meals.
6 Government-owned hotels in Spain. 7 A menu
with a wide choice of dishes. 8 A menu with a fixed
price and limited choice.

79   **Strange railway**

1 Sleepers do not have chairs. 2 Left-hand track:
two sleepers are on top of the rail. 3 Right-hand
track: one sleeper is short. 4 Left-hand signal is
positioned wrongly. 5 Right-hand signal: the two
arms should be positioned separately. 6 The train
is not running on a set of rails. 7 The overhead
electric wires are missing. 8 The signal box faces
the wrong way. 9 The clock has only eleven
numerals. 10 The luggage trolley has lost a wheel.
11 The waiting room signs are blank. 12 The foot-
bridge does not continue across the track but stops
in mid-air.

Famous cars

1 Model T Ford. 2 Jaguar XJ6. 3 VW Beetle.
4 Bullnose Morris. 5 Morris Mini. 6 Rolls-Royce
Silver Ghost. 7 Citroen DS. 8 Hillman Minx. 9 MG
Midget. 10 Rover 80.

82 **International time**

A 1 7 am. 2 3 pm. 3 4 am. 4 5.30 pm. 5 12 noon.
6 3.30 pm. 7 8 pm. 8 2 pm. 9 10 pm. 10 7.30 pm.
11 9 am. 12 12 midnight (i.e., following).
B 1 10 am. 2 2 am. 3 5 pm. 4 4 pm. 5 Midnight.
6 4 pm. 7 3 pm. 8 12.30 pm.

83 **Air knowledge**

1 (a) The BAC 1-11 is the only three-engined aircraft; the others have four. (b) The BAC Vanguard
is a prop-jet, while the others are pure jets.
2 International Air Transport Association; it regu-
lates the standards, fares and conduct of the airlines
throughout the world which belong to it. 3 London (Heathrow, Gatwick), Manchester, Glasgow,
Edinburgh, Bristol, Belfast, Aberdeen, Birmingham, Leeds/Bradford, Exeter, Bournemouth, Car-
diff, Southend, Norwich, Newcastle. 4 Los Angeles
(LAX), London (LON), Sydney (SYD), Ankara
(ANK), Paris (PAR), Johannesburg (JNB), Buenos
Aires (BUE), Glasgow (GLA), Moscow (MOW),

Bombay (BOM), Warsaw (WAW), Nairobi (NBO).
5 Sir Frank Whittle. 6 Avtur 3. 7 (a) 3456 miles,
(b) 688 miles, (c) 2204 miles, (d) 1385 miles, (e)
4184 miles, (f) 6259 miles, (g) 2397 miles.

84/85 Railway signals and signs

1 Maximum speed permitted. 2 Danger – overhead
live wires. 3 Temporary speed restriction. 4 Gradi-
ent ahead. 5 Sound the whistle. 6 Catch points
ahead. 7 The head code.

86 Knowing London

1 The Mall.   2 (a) Victoria, (b) Charing Cross,
(c) Waterloo, (d) Liverpool Street, (e) Euston,
(f) Euston, (g) King's Cross, (h) Paddington. 3 It is
a special ticket which enables you to travel as
much as you like on London's red buses in one
day. 4 Westminster Bridge and Lambeth Bridge.
5 Science, Natural History, Geological, Victoria and
Albert. 6 Regent's Park. 7 Bond Street, Regent
Street, Oxford Street and Piccadilly. 8 Tower
Bridge. 9 620 feet; for handling telephone and television signals. 10 The Oval and Lord's. 11 Apsley
House, the home of the Duke of Wellington.
12 At Madame Tussaud's, the world famous
waxworks. 13 Oliver Cromwell's statue is by
Westminster Hall and it faces a carved head of
Charles I above a doorway of St Margaret's Church.

87   **Famous arches**

1 Arc de Triomphe, Paris. **2** Admiralty Arch, London. **3** Arch of Constantine, Rome. **4** Brandenburg Gate, Berlin. **5** Marble Arch, London.

88   **Motoring safety**

The Highway Code is issued by the Government and offers rules and advice on travelling safely on the roads. Drivers must know it as part of their driving test. **1** Red, amber and green. **2** Red; red and amber; green; amber; red. **3** It means you can go in the direction shown by the arrow. **4** Because children may run out from behind it. **5** To slow down and stop as a vehicle has stopped ahead for an emergency. **6** Brakes, tyres, lamps and reflectors. **7** Yes, unless road markings indicate otherwise. **8** Stop at the kerb, look right, look left, look right again. When the road is clear, walk across at right angles but keep looking out for traffic. Cross the road as quickly as you can, but do not run. **9** All the time; to reduce the chance of being thrown around in the car and suffering injury in an accident or emergency stop. **10** A crash-helmet.

89   **Navigation help**

1 Lighthouse. **2** Starboard-hand buoy. **3** Port-hand buoy. **4** Wreck buoy. **5** Middle ground buoy. **6** Lightship.

90/91 Parts of vehicles

1 Boeing 707 tail. 2 Citroen DS front. 3 QE2 funnel. 4 Front of a Mercedes coach. 5 Hawker Siddeley Trident tail. 6 Rear end of a BLMC Mini. 7 Stern of a cross-channel ferry. 8 Part of a hovercraft skirt. 9 Concorde nose. 10 Forward cabin of a Boeing 747.

92 Oceans and seas

A 1 English Channel. 2 Mediterranean Sea. 3 Indian Ocean. 4 Red Sea. 5 Baltic Sea. 6 Atlantic Ocean. 7 Pacific Ocean. 8 East China Sea. 9 Black Sea. B Caspian Sea, Aral Sea, Dead Sea. C 1 Between South American mainland and Tierra del Fuego. 2 Between Malaysia and Singapore island. 3 Between Caernarvonshire and Anglesey. 4 Between Australia and Tasmania. 5 Between Alaska and USSR. 6 Between Spain and North Africa.

93 Road travel

1 Italy; chariots and other horse-drawn vehicles. 2 (a) Scotland, (b) USSR. 3 RAC 'Old Crocks' race. 4 *A Tale of Two Cities*; Mr Jarvis Lorry. 5 A highwayman. 6 Charing Cross. 7 They are the names of Roman roads in Britain. 8 Thomas Telford, John Loudon McAdam, John Metcalf (Blind Jack of Knaresborough). 9 A road which you paid to travel

on. 10 Rome. 11 (a) A person who drives selfishly and recklessly, (b) an American bird, the chaparral cock, (c) a roller, such as a steam-roller, for crushing and smoothing the surface.

94/95 **World capitals**

1 Washington DC. 2 Mexico City. 3 Brasilia. 4 Buenos Aires. 5 London. 6 Madrid. 7 Oslo. 8 Warsaw. 9 Moscow. 10 Rome. 11 Pretoria. 12 Delhi. 13 Bangkok. 14 Tokyo. 15 Canberra.

Space for spotters

Note here the international registration letters for vehicles.

Your travel mileage

Note here the distance between the places you visit and total up your holiday mileage. You may be surprised how far you travel.

From	To	Distance

More Beaver Books

We hope you have enjoyed this Beaver Book. Here are some of the other titles:

A Knight and his Castle   What it was like to live in a castle, by R. Ewart Oakeshott

The Twelve Labours of Hercules   The adventures of the hero Hercules, beautifully retold by Robert Newman; illustrated superbly by Charles Keeping

My Favourite Animal Stories   Sad, funny and exciting stories about all sorts of animals, chosen and introduced by Gerald Durrell

Who Knows?   Twelve unsolved mysteries involving sudden death, mysterious disappearances and hidden treasure, by Jacynth Hope-Simpson

The Call of the Wild   The epic story of Buck the great sledge dog in the frozen North, by Jack London

The Last of the Vikings   Henry Treece's exciting story, in the saga tradition, about the young Harald Hardrada, King of Norway; with more superb illustrations by Charles Keeping

Ghost Horse   Dramatic story about a legendary stallion in the American West, by Joseph E. Chipperfield

New Beavers are published every month and if you would like the *Beaver Bulletin* – which gives all the details – please send a stamped addressed envelope to:

Beaver Bulletin
The Hamlyn Group
Astronaut House
Feltham
Middlesex TW14 9AR

387402